NATIONAL
GEOGRAPHIC
KiDS

101 LiFE HACKS

Genius Ways to Simplify Your World

NATIONAL GEOGRAPHIC
WASHINGTON, D.C.

WHAT THE HACK?

A life hack is a clever trick or shortcut that makes an ordinary task easier. Hacks can save you time, help you grow smarter or stronger, and even help save the planet. But some hacks are just plain fun!

Find out the best way to eat a cupcake. And the fastest way to fall asleep. Want to learn how to draw a perfect circle? Or how to multiply big numbers in your head? In this book, you'll find a life hack for just about anything—from homework to chores to dessert.

When it comes down to it, life hacking is all about solving a problem in a creative way. That's why throughout this book we've included cool stories about incredible inventors and innovators. They turned their hacks into gadgets that are now used by people all over the world. After all, the best part of life hacking is sharing your awesome new skills with other people. And who knows? You may even come up with some life hacks of your own. (Turn to page 196 for help on that.)

HAPPY HACKING!

LOOK AROUND YOU

Many hacks use items that you already have in your home—but in clever ways. See if the things you already own can serve a new purpose. In time, you'll think twice about throwing something useful away or buying something new that you just don't need. Check out these ways to give old stuff a new life:

➡️ **Reuse:**
To use something again or in a new way. For example, when you wrap your sandwich in a bandanna and then also use the bandanna as a napkin. (Turn to page 138!)

➡️ **Recycle:**
To convert waste into reusable material, like when you turn scrap paper into beads. (Turn to page 14!)

➡️ **Repurpose:**
To give something a new purpose, like when you use a carabiner to hold hair ties. (Turn to page 135!)

➡️ **Upcycle:**
To create something of high value from an object of lesser value, like when you turn an empty bottle into a sprinkler. (Turn to page 170!)

kids  PLASTIC

Why is reusing, repurposing, and upcycling important?
We rely on single-use plastic products and packaging—like straws, juice pouches, and containers—too much. It's estimated that seven billion tons (6.4 t) of that plastic sit in landfills or pollute Earth's oceans. (That's about the same weight as a billion *T. rex!*) As if that wasn't bad enough, the simple act of making plastic causes pollution. If we consume less and reuse more, it will be better for the environment—and in turn better for us!

YOU'RE EATING IT WRONG!

Try these easier, less messy ways to devour some of your favorite foods.

There's nothing better than a frozen ice pop on a hot summer day. Before you step into the sun, poke your ice pop stick through a cupcake liner. *Voilà!* Now you've got a drip tray to catch the melting madness. So long, sticky hands!

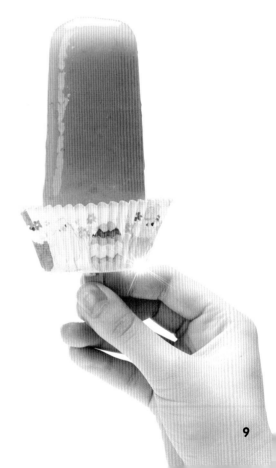

Next time you grab a banana, flip it over and peel it from the bottom.

Just pinch the end and then start pulling.
(It's easier. We're not monkeying around!)

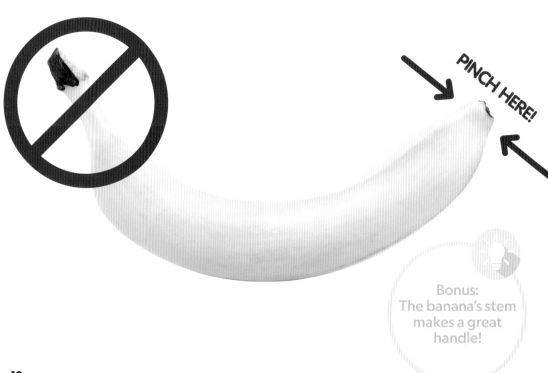

PINCH HERE!

Bonus:
The banana's stem
makes a great
handle!

Rebuild your cupcake into a handheld sandwich that keeps your fingers—and your face—frosting free.

1 Remove the cupcake liner.

2 Hold the cupcake with two hands and gently pull the bottom half away from the top of the cake.

3 Press the bottom half on top of the frosting to create a cupcake sandwich.

4 Eat and enjoy!

SECRET STORAGE

The perfect spot to keep your stuff safe is hidden in plain sight!

 4 **Reuse old plastic containers.** Clean them out and hide your valuables inside!

An empty lip balm container is a great place to store a rolled-up dollar bill in your backpack.

5 **Plastic eggs** are *egg*-cellent for storing small things like jewelry or headphones. If you have any hanging around the house, think of new ways to use them.

PAPER
NOT PLASTIC

6 **Repurpose the piles of paper already in your home—by turning them into art!** Junk mail, magazines, and newspaper scraps can become beautiful beads with a little bit of cutting and rolling.

(Be sure to ask an adult for permission first!)

Scrap paper

Scissors

Dowel
(a pencil or straw will work, too)

Glue

Craft sealer
(optional)

Cut a very tall triangle shape out of your scrap paper. The wide end will become the final width of the bead.

15

Starting with the wide end, roll the paper tightly around the dowel.

Add a line of glue to the pointy end, continue to roll the paper, and then hold it together for a few seconds until the glue dries.

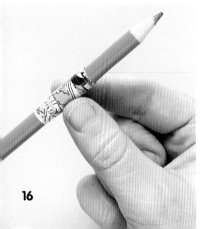

Optional: Finish the bead with a coat of sealer. Let it dry overnight. Then remove the bead from the dowel.

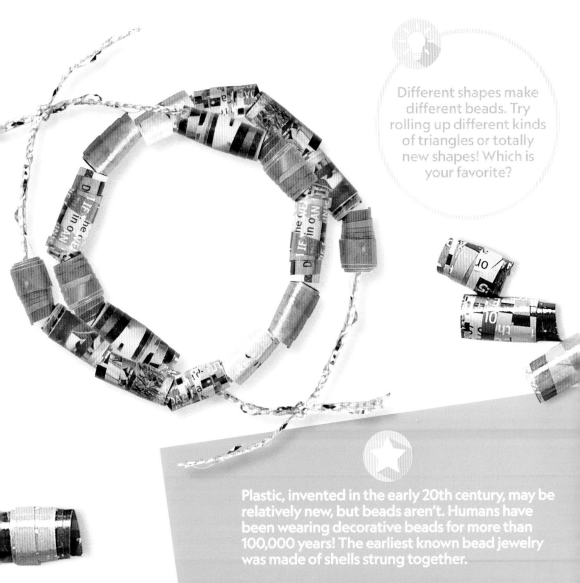

Different shapes make different beads. Try rolling up different kinds of triangles or totally new shapes! Which is your favorite?

Plastic, invented in the early 20th century, may be relatively new, but beads aren't. Humans have been wearing decorative beads for more than 100,000 years! The earliest known bead jewelry was made of shells strung together.

HACKER HERO

Hacker: Topher White

Invention: A monitoring device that helps save the rainforest

Engineer Topher White knew that forests around the world were disappearing fast—and that it was a big problem for the animals that lived there. But he didn't know that fewer forests were bad for the environment, too. Deforestation, which is the removal of trees from a certain area, is a huge contributor to climate change—even more than the exhaust from all the cars around the world.

Much of the time, people cut down rainforest trees illegally. Topher wanted to create a way to find these people and stop them. He had a simple idea: He took an old cell phone, and

then added a microphone and attached solar panels to keep it charged. Then he put his creation up in a tree and listened. It worked! His device could pick up chain-saw sounds from a mile away and send a signal to other cell phones on the ground. On just his second day of testing, Topher stopped illegal loggers from cutting down trees in a forest in Indonesia!

Now Topher's monitoring devices have been used around the world to help stop deforestation. When a device detects the noise of a chain saw, it sends a text message to authorities who can investigate. Not only is he saving the planet, he's repurposing an everyday item (that often ends up in the trash) to help change the world. It's a win-win for everyone!

HACK YOUR HOMEWORK

These tips will help you stay focused and get organized, so you can sail through school like a pro.

**Need to study for a big test?
Or finish a math assignment?**

Try the Pomodoro Technique. Set an alarm clock for 25 minutes. Now work, work, work until the alarm goes off. Then reward yourself with five minutes of free time. Need more time? Set the alarm again for another round.

Why It Works

Working in short, uninterrupted sprints and rewarding yourself afterward is a great way to stay focused. The time limit gives you a sense of urgency, so you feel like you have to get your work done faster. The five-minute breaks give your brain a much needed rest, so you can recharge and then get back to work.

8 **Leave the first page of your notebook blank.** Use it as a running table of contents instead. You'll add to it as you fill in your notes.

Contents

1.

2.

3.

4.

First you'll have to number each page of your notebook in the top or bottom corner. Then use the table of contents to track what's on which pages—like when you started taking notes on a new topic or chapter. You'll be able to find the important stuff more easily when you study.

It might feel silly, but before you turn in a paper, read it out loud to yourself. It may help you catch errors and even improve your grade!

Why It Works

Writing pros believe that mistakes are easier to spot when you're listening instead of reading silently. It's easier to hear some problems than to see them, such as run-on sentences or missing and repeated words.

DON'T FORGET TO FLOSS!

This sweet trick isn't quite what your dentist had in mind.

10

Cut a cake with unflavored dental floss instead of a knife. Bakers love this trick because you can evenly cut a cake into smooth slices or layers! Most knives aren't as long as a cake—but a piece of floss can be as long as you need it to be, so you'll be able to create perfectly straight lines.

It's simple: Wrap a long length of floss (a few inches longer than the cake on each side) a couple of times around your fingers. Then slowly pull it downward through the cake. Wipe the floss clean after each "cut."

OWNING
YOUR IDEAS

When people have great ideas of their own, they can make it official by getting a patent. In the United States, inventors have been patenting their ideas for hundreds of years!

➡ **What's a patent, anyway?**
A patent is a license that proves you created something unique. It's a form of protection for your invention. When you own a patent, you're the only one who can make and sell that invention until the patent runs out—usually in 14 or 20 years.

➡ **Can anything be patented?**
Nope. There are rules to what can and cannot be patented. It must be something completely unique and very different from existing inventions. You also have to show how your invention works and that it is useful in some way.

➡ **Who can get a patent?**
Anyone with a good idea. But it'll cost you. A patent for even the most simple invention can cost thousands of dollars!

Inventions are everywhere—even in your own bathroom. Inventor Seth Wheeler secured the patent for the toilet paper roll in 1891.

Abraham Lincoln is the only U.S. president to hold a patent. He created a system to help riverboats float over sandbars.

In 1984, Frances Gabe received a patent for her self-cleaning house—including dishwashing cupboards and nozzles to spray down the walls.

CRUSH WATER WASTE

Help save water—and the planet—with these smart tricks.

DITCH WASTEFUL DISH WASHING.

Believe it or not, dishwashing machines actually use less energy and water than handwashing. Scrape the food from your plates (instead of rinsing them), and then load up the dishwasher. Run it only when it's full.

If you don't have a dishwasher, fill up half the sink (or one large bowl) with soapy water and the other half of the sink (or another large bowl) with water for rinsing. You'll use about half as much water than if you let the sink run!

TRICK OUT YOUR TOILET.

12

Reuse a half-gallon milk jug or plastic water bottle. Put sand or small rocks inside to weigh it down, and then top it off with water and close the bottle. Ask an adult to place it in the tank of your toilet away from any moving parts. Now the water bottle takes up room in your toilet tank that new water would have had to fill.

13

HOLD
THE HOSE.

When you have to wash the family car or clean up your bike, don't just grab the hose. Instead, fill up a bucket with water and use a sponge to scrub it clean. When you let the hose run, you're using (and losing) way more water than you actually need.

14 JUST RELAX!

It's moments before you take the stage or hop on a scary roller coaster. Your palms are sweaty, and your heart is beating superfast. **Try this breathing exercise to calm yourself down:**

1

Place one hand on your chest and one hand on your belly.

2

Breathe in deeply through your nose. Your belly will fill with air and push your hand outward. The hand on your chest should stay still.

3

As if you're whistling, blow the air out of your mouth. Now the hand on your belly will move inward.

4

Repeat three to 10 more times.

HACKER HERO

Hacker: Caine Monroy

Invention: Caine's Arcade

His dad's auto parts store was filled with empty boxes, but nine-year-old Caine Monroy saw something else. He worked for days on end during his summer break. Before long, an arcade made using only cardboard, scissors, tape, and old toys had seemingly grown out of nothing. Caine's dad was shocked.

A small basketball hoop taped to a box became a hoops game, green army soldiers acted as goalies for a soccer game, and an S-hook and yarn became his own claw machine. He cut a slot into the front of each box, so he could push

tickets through when people won. The finishing touches? Prizes taped to the wall and a homemade T-shirt that read "Caine's Arcade."

The Global Cardboard Challenge honors Caine's Arcade by hosting an annual Day of Play that encourages kids to get creative with cardboard.

A filmmaker happened to walk into the auto store to buy something for his car. Caine's first customer had arrived! The filmmaker thought Caine's Arcade was so cool that he decided to make a short film about it and tell his friends to check it out. Soon, a huge line had formed outside the arcade that stretched around the block. There was a four-hour-long wait to get in!

At the same time, kids all over the world started sending videos of their own cardboard creations—from pinball machines to Skee-Ball games—to Caine. Caine's Arcade had become an inspiration. When other people just saw an old box, Caine saw something more. That's a true sign of an inventor—thinking outside the box (literally)!

YOU'RE MAGNETIC

These hacks will attract attention!

Always looking for something to write with?

Glue a magnet to a plastic cup. (Make sure the magnet is wide enough so that it juts out past the lip of the cup.) Then stick it to a locker or refrigerator. Instant pencil holder!

kids vs. PLASTIC

Next time you use a plastic cup, don't throw it away. Give it a good wash and put your imagination to the test. What else can you do with it?

Never lose your keys again! Hang a ring magnet to a key ring with a short piece of ribbon or string. Now you can attach your keys to your locker at school or the refrigerator at home.

What you'll need:

Ribbon

Scissors

Ring magnet
(found at hardware stores and online)

1 Cut a 1/4-inch (0.6 cm) ribbon 10 inches (25 cm) long. Fold it in half.

2 Push the folded end through the center of the magnet.

3 Loop the folded end around the loose ends and pull.

4 Tie the loose ends in a knot and hang it from your key chain.

Ever lost your place because a bookmark slipped out? A magnetic bookmark will stay in place—and it can mark the exact sentence you're on!

What you'll need:

Thick paper
(like scrapbook paper or an old folder)

Scissors

Adhesive magnetic sheet
(found at craft stores and online)

**Optional:
Stickers or markers
for decoration**

1

Cut the paper into a rectangle about 1.5 inches (4 cm) wide by 6 inches (15 cm) long. Now fold it in half.

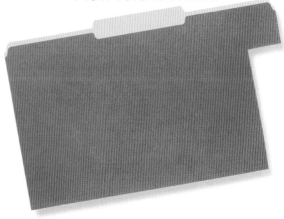

2

Cut an adhesive magnet sheet into two rectangles about 1 inch (2.5 cm) wide by 2 inches (5 cm) long.

3

Attach the magnets to the inside top and bottom of the folded paper.

4

Decorate your bookmark with stickers, markers, or whatever you want!

WHEN LIFE GIVES YOU
CAKE MIX

Lemons can make lemonade, and
cake mix can make ... cookies?
Find out how!

18

You heard us right: With just a couple of ingredients, you can turn a box of cake mix into cookie dough.

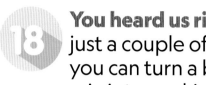

Always ask an adult for help when you're working in the kitchen—especially when using an oven.

You'll need:

1 box of cake mix (any flavor)

1/3 cup (80 mL) oil

2 eggs

1 Pour the premade cake mix into a bowl.

2 Add the eggs and oil. Beat with an electric hand mixer.

3 Roll dough into one-inch (2.5-cm) balls. Place on cookie sheet.

4 Bake for 8–10 minutes at 350°F (177°C).

THE CHEMISTRY BEHIND
COOKIE DOUGH

Did you know that baking is science? Delicious science! Every ingredient in dough is there for a reason.
Let's break it down:

Butter (or oil) gives the cookie flavor and keeps it soft. It also helps the cookie spread as it warms in the oven.

Baking soda reacts with sugar and melted butter to make the cookie rise.

Eggs add moisture to help dissolve the sugar.

Cake mix usually calls for water, eggs, and oil in order to make it moist, fluffy, and spongy. By removing the water and cutting down the number of eggs, the end result is drier but still soft, sweet, and chewy— a perfect cookie!

Sugar makes the cookie sweet. Brown sugar makes a softer, taller cookie than white sugar, which makes a thinner, crisper cookie.

Flour helps the cookie keep its shape. Cake flour, like the cake mix in the recipe on page 43, makes slightly softer cookies.

45

ON-THE-GO HACKS

These travel tips will help you go far—literally!

A reusable shower cap makes a great cover for dirty shoes when you're packing. (Just make sure you wash it before you use it for your hair!)

20

DIY your own TV

and you'll be able to watch your favorite shows hands free from a plane or a car.

A sandwich-size bag will work for most phones, and a gallon-size bag will work for most tablets.

What you'll need:
Resealable bag

Duct tape or masking tape

Hole punch

Ribbon or yarn

1 Attach a piece of tape along the front top edge of the bag, just under the zipper seal. Leave 1 inch (2.5 cm) of tape hanging on each side to create a tab.

2 Now attach a piece of tape along the back top edge, lining it up with the first piece of tape, so all the sticky stuff is covered.

3

Use the hole punch to punch a circle through the tape tabs on each side of the bag. String ribbon or yarn through the holes and tie each end into a double knot.

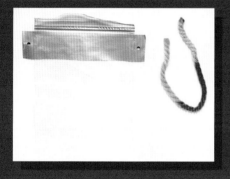

4

Slip a phone or tablet into the bag. Now hang it from the knob of the tray holder on an airplane or around the headrest of the seat in front of you in the car.

If you need to use a plastic bag in your lunch, wash it afterward. Then try to think of ways you can reuse or repurpose it!

21 Roll up your clothes to make more room in your stuffed suitcase. Want even more convenience? You can layer complete outfits together and roll them up to create a grab-and-go look!

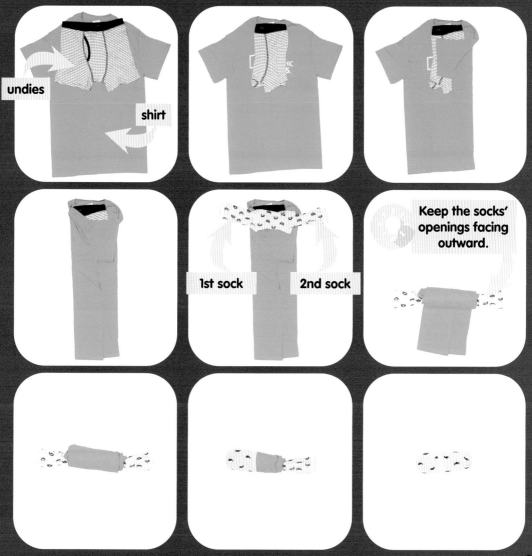

undies

shirt

1st sock   2nd sock

Keep the socks' openings facing outward.

JOINED AT
THE CLIP

Binder clips aren't just for holding papers together! These super-simple hacks will seriously organize your life.

22 **Turn a binder clip into a wallet or even a key chain.** Secure folded dollar bills with the clip, and then attach a key ring to the arms of the clip.

23

Don't let any toothpaste go unused.

Roll up the bottom of a toothpaste tube, and then attach a binder clip.
Bonus: It doubles as a stand!

24

Use binder clips to keep cords from getting tangled.

Louis E. Baltzley invented binder clips in 1911. But Louis wasn't the only inventor in the family: His grandfather created the first sewing machine. And his dad and uncle held 10 patents for inventions, too!

LIGHT BRIGHT

25 Make an emergency lamp!

Turn on your cell phone's flashlight, and then set it under a translucent reusable bottle filled with water to make a handy lantern. Or attach a headlamp around a jug of water (with the light facing inward toward the water). Now watch the water glow!

Why It Works

When you strap your headlamp to the water jug, some of its light waves enter the water and bounce off the water molecules in all different directions. The light scatters during this process—called diffusion—creating a nice glow, rather than a single beam of light.

A BETTER BANDAGE

26 Does your bandage keep slipping off your finger? One snip at each end will help it stay on.

What you'll need:

Bandage
Scissors

If you've hurt yourself, be sure to go to an adult for help first!

56

Make a horizontal snip into each end of the bandage.

Place the bandage on your finger.

Wrap the bottom corners and top corners inward diagonally.

WHAT IS AN ENGINEER?

Inventors aren't the only people who create new ideas.

Engineers are like life-hackers on a huge scale! They build bridges to hack their way over rivers and build tunnels to hack through mountains. They design machines, structures, and products that make our lives way easier. Without engineers, our cities wouldn't run as smoothly as they do now.

There are lots of different kinds of engineers, from chemical engineers to computer engineers to mechanical engineers. But they all have something in common: They are very curious! Engineers are known to take something apart just to see how it works and put it back together again.

Engineers have a tried-and-true problem-solving process. Once they identify a problem to tackle, they brainstorm a bunch of different solutions. After a lot of consideration, they choose the best one. Then they create a plan, which usually involves building a model or a prototype to make sure their plan works. If it doesn't—no worries—they go back to the drawing board!

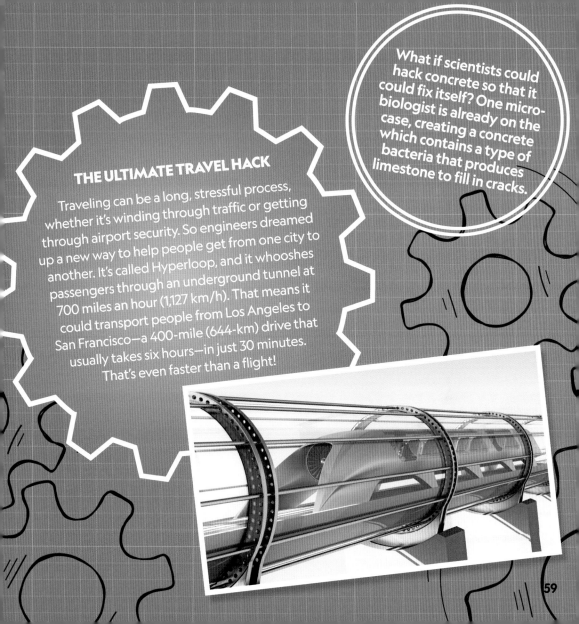

What if scientists could hack concrete so that it could fix itself? One microbiologist is already on the case, creating a concrete which contains a type of bacteria that produces limestone to fill in cracks.

THE ULTIMATE TRAVEL HACK

Traveling can be a long, stressful process, whether it's winding through traffic or getting through airport security. So engineers dreamed up a new way to help people get from one city to another. It's called Hyperloop, and it whooshes passengers through an underground tunnel at 700 miles an hour (1,127 km/h). That means it could transport people from Los Angeles to San Francisco—a 400-mile (644-km) drive that usually takes six hours—in just 30 minutes. That's even faster than a flight!

CHOP, CHOP!

Make disposable chopsticks easier to use.

All you need is the paper wrapper they come in and a rubber band. Stack the chopsticks, and then wrap the rubber band tightly around the thicker ends. Now roll the wrapper tightly and insert it between the two chopsticks near the rubber band.

Why It Works

Chopsticks are a type of simple machine called a lever. In this case, the rolled-up paper acts as the lever's fulcrum. In physics, a fulcrum is the point at which something is balanced or supported. Thanks to your fulcrum (or paper), you have to move your fingers only slightly to get a wide range of motion to pick up a tiny grain of rice or a whole sushi roll.

One way to use chopsticks is to hold the top chopstick as if you were holding a pencil. The bottom chopstick goes under your thumb and rests between your middle and ring finger.

START A SPARK!

28

You don't have to be a wilderness pro to build a roaring fire. You can make a simple fire starter with potato chips. Ask an adult to place a handful into the center of your fire and drop a match on top.

Why It Works

Potato chips are thinly sliced potatoes that are fried in oil. Because they are high in fat, and fat burns easily, they catch fire quickly.

Always grab an adult when you want to get a toasty campfire started.

MASTER YOUR MEMORY

Here are a few brain-boosting tips to help you remember stuff.

29

Create mnemonic devices—phrases that are easy to remember and remind you of something else. They're like shortcuts for your brain! It's simple: The first letter in each word corresponds to the letter of something more difficult that you're trying to memorize.

 TRY IT!

The names of the planets are (in order from the sun)

Mercury, Venus, Earth, Mars, Jupiter, Saturn, Uranus, and Neptune.

To help you recall this order, remember this funny phrase:

My Very Educated Mother Just Served Us Nachos.

30 Need to memorize a series of facts or items on a list? Walk through your "memory palace" and you'll be able to recall them easily. It's a trick that competitive memory champions use.

TRY IT!

Think of a common route in your home, like your walk from the front door to your bedroom. Now imagine five or 10 items you need to memorize. Mentally "place" those items at important stops along the route.

When you need to remember these items, "walk" through your memory palace route in your head. The visuals that appear along your walk should help you recall things more easily.

Why It Works

Scientists have found that we remember pictures better than words. So when you imagine your home with items inside of it (rather than a list of words), you may be able to recall them more easily.

When memorizing vocabulary words, trivia, or dates, write them down over and over again. But don't just copy them. Make yourself recall the information on your own each time you write them down. Then you'll know exactly which items you're stumbling over and can focus more time on teaching yourself those facts.

Some memory experts believe you have to recall something 30 times before it's memorized.

32

Sing! Try singing facts you need to memorize to a familiar tune like "Happy Birthday," "Mary Had a Little Lamb," or the "Alphabet Song."

Memorable Music

Brain scientists believe that when information is set to familiar music, it's much easier to remember. The rhythm and rhyme of song lyrics provide a structure, and the melody acts as a cue, or a signal, to your brain. That's why you sometimes have to sing a song instead of just speaking it in order to remember the words.

Music also helps us use a memory trick called "chunking." Think of the "Alphabet Song." Instead of remembering 26 separate pieces of information, the song helps us group the letters into fewer chunks of information. "L-M-N-O-P" rolls right off our tongues as if it's one piece of information. It's a no-brainer: Fewer things are easier to remember than more things!

LEND A HAND

33 Use your fingers to estimate how many more minutes of daylight you have based on the setting sun.

Here's How It Works

Extend your arm directly in front of you. Bend your hand so that your palm faces you. Now place the bottom of your pinkie finger in line with the horizon. Count how many fingers come between the sun and the horizon. Each finger represents about 15 minutes. You can use your other hand, too, if you need to!

1 hour

45 minutes

30 minutes

15 minutes

horizon

71

IN THE
BAG

 34 Make your own gift bag out of wrapping paper.

What you'll need:

Stack of books or
empty box
(to use as a form)

Wrapping paper

Glue

Tape

Hole punch

Ribbon or string

1

Use a stack of books or an empty box as a form for your bag. Set your form in the center bottom of a length of wrapping paper (pattern side facing down).

2

Cut the wrapping paper so that it's large enough to cover your form in both width and height.

3

Choose one side to be the top of your bag. Fold the edge inward and glue it in place.

4 Wrap the paper inward around the form and secure the seam with tape. (Don't wrap too tightly!)

5 Wrap the bottom of the form as if you were wrapping a gift. Secure it with tape.

6 Use the hole punch to create holes at the top of the bag. Add a handle by looping a ribbon or string through the holes on each side and tying double knots at both ends.

Some gift bags are coated with a clear layer of plastic, or are made entirely of plastic. Plastic is hard to recycle, which is why this paper gift bag is much more eco-friendly.

HACKER HERO

Hacker: Karen DeMatteo

Invention: A new way to research a little-known animal

It's hard to believe that there could be an animal out there that we don't know a lot about. But it's true, even with today's technology! So when one biologist wanted to research the rare bush dog in South America, she had to get creative.

Karen DeMatteo knew that a forest in Argentina was becoming threatened due to more roads, more humans, and more buildings. That meant the animals that lived there, like the bush dog, needed to be protected. But there was just one problem—she didn't know much about the animal. She could barely even capture a photo of the little critter. Since humans and technology couldn't seem to get the job done, Karen turned to a different helper—a furry one.

Train is a detection dog. He uses his sense of smell to detect the scent of the bush dog. Human noses aren't nearly as strong as dog noses are. Thanks to Train's hard work, Karen was able to conduct the first major study of the bush dog. And with that information, she could help better protect the land and the bush dogs who lived on it. Now that's a creative way to help—from one furry friend to another!

SOUND OFF!

35 Use a tall drinking glass or a glass bowl as a speaker for a phone. Just plop it in and rock on.

Why It Works

The drinking glass creates something called an echo chamber. It's a space where sound echoes, or repeats, because it is reflected off walls. When this happens, the sound becomes amplified, or louder.

START
SNOOZZZzzING!

Fall asleep faster with these tricks.

36

Take a warm shower or bath about an hour before your bedtime.

Why It Works

A drop in body temperature signals to your body it's time for bed. The water from a warm shower or bath exaggerates this signal. Your body heats up while you're in the steamy bathroom, but when you step into your cooler bedroom, your body temperature drops. Then your body starts slowing down everything—from your heart rate to your digestion. Before you know it, you'll be snoozing!

37

Slip on some warm socks so your feet don't freeze!

Cold feet could prevent you from falling asleep—or wake you up in the middle of the night. But warming them up can help you get some shut-eye.

Why It Works

When you heat up your freezing tootsies, your blood vessels dilate—or become larger. And that's a bedtime signal for your brain. Some researchers believe that the sooner your feet and hands warm up, the sooner you will drift off to dreamland.

38

Grab a book before you hop into bed and start reading.

Why It Works

Reading is a major stress-reducer, and it's easier to sleep when you're relaxed. It will help calm you down and prepare your body for a night of good sleep. (Just make sure you're reading a paper book: The artificial light from tablets and phones can trick your brain into thinking it's not bedtime, no matter how comfy you are!)

SCREEN STAND

39 A pair of sunglasses can double as an instant cell phone stand. Now you can watch videos without your phone falling.

COOL & COZY

40

Keep cold drinks cool—and your hands warm—with an upcycled drink cozy. All you need is one old, hole-y sock and a pair of scissors. Snip off the bottom of the sock below the ankle. Then slip the rest over your bottle of choice. (Note: You'll probably want to wash the sock first.)

SHOW YOUR SHIRTS

41

Tired of digging for your favorite tee?

Display your folded T-shirts vertically.
That way you can see them all instantly
when you open your drawer.

1 Lay your shirt flat.

2 Fold it in half vertically.

3 Fold the sleeves inward.

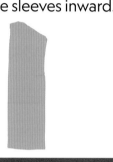

4 Fold the shirt in half horizontally.

5 Fold it in half one more time.

TRAIN YOUR BRAIN!

These tips make your brain stronger and healthier over time. They're great exercise for your mind and a good way to hack yourself into becoming a smarter person.

42 Pick up an instrument.

When playing music, your brain has to process all kinds of things—sight, sound, touch, and fine movements—at the same time. Talk about a mental workout! The structure of musicians' brains changes—causing certain brain areas to be larger than those in non-musicians. Musicians often have improved brain skills, such as a strong working memory—the skill that helps you keep numbers in your head as you do mental math.

Hola

Privyet

43

Learn a new language.

Studies have found that people who are bilingual can often remember things more easily and jump from one task to another more quickly. Learning a second language can even increase the size of your brain!

Ciao

Hei

44

Exercise your body.

It turns out that exercising your body is an exercise for your mind, too! The more active you are, the healthier your brain will be. Exercise increases blood flow to the brain, giving it the oxygen and nutrients it needs to stay fit. With only about an hour of activity a day, you could understand things more quickly and improve your memory!

HACKER HERO

Hacker: Arthur Huang

Invention: A charger with a zero carbon footprint

Engineer Arthur Huang knows saving the planet isn't just about recycling. It's about minimizing our carbon footprints. That means reducing the amount of greenhouse gases you release into the environment each day. You might start by using less electricity at home, walking instead of driving, or composting your trash.

It's easier to reduce your carbon footprint when the items you use every day aren't creating greenhouse gases. Arthur knew that we could make products with no carbon footprint, so that's what he set out to do. His first product was a hand-held device that looks like a portable fan. It uses the wind, the

sun, or a hand crank to collect energy, which can then power up your phone or tablet. No electricity needed! But he didn't stop there—it was even made from recycled plastic waste from electronics!

Arthur continues to make products like this today and is a big advocate for upcycling on a huge scale. He wants to shape a world where we take old things that we already have and repurpose them into something new—over and over again. Arthur's creative thinking is good for the environment and good for us!

PANCAKE LIKE A PRO

45

Pour pancake mix into an empty squeeze bottle. (You can repurpose a washed-out ketchup or mustard bottle.) Now you can make perfect-size pancakes with less mess!

Pack one of these premade-pancake-mix squeeze bottles in a cooler the next time you go camping.

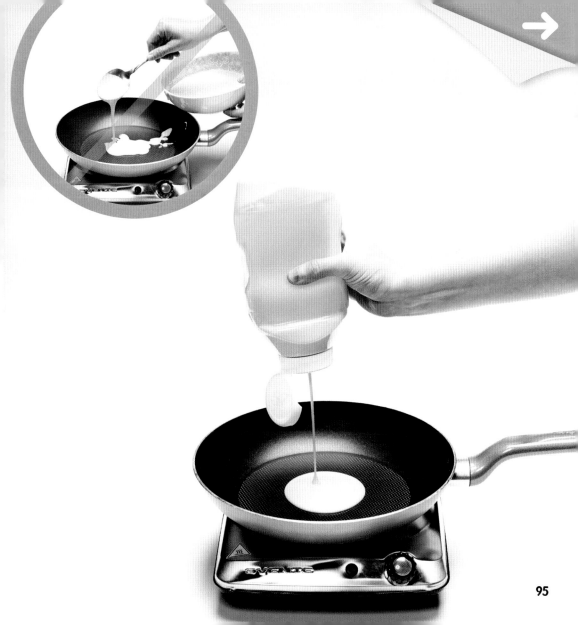

Want to step up your pancake game even more?

Separate your pancake mix into a few different small bowls. Then add a couple of drops of food coloring or cocoa powder to each one and stir.

If you're feeling especially artistic, try squeezing words or shapes onto the pan. Here are some ideas:

Create a polka-dot pattern with multiple colors.

Go wild! Make a wacky abstract design.

Make a smiley face with two different colors.

Make a swirl with two different colors.

THAT STINKS!

Repel bad smells with these hacks.

46

Afraid you have bad breath? Lick the inside of your wrist, wait a moment, and smell it to check.

47 Here's a super-simple solution for your stinky bedroom: Put some vanilla extract on a cotton ball. Then leave the ball on a small dish close to where the funky smell seems to be coming from. It's a natural air freshener!

48 Put a scented dryer sheet inside a pair of smelly shoes. You'll feel better with each step knowing that your feet smell fresh.

49

No dryer sheets? No problem! You can also conquer shoe stink with baking soda. Simply leave some in your shoes overnight. (Just don't forget to empty out the leftover powder before you slip them on in the morning!)

Baking soda is so useful that it even has its own holiday: National Bicarbonate of Soda Day, on December 30th!

MATH MAGIC

Your friends will think you're a math whiz when you solve these complex problems in a snap.

Add triple digits in your head by breaking them down into simpler sums. Add the 100s column, then the 10s, and then the 1s. Then add them all together!

621 + 374 = ?

600 + 300 = 900
20 + 70 = 90
1 + 4 = 5

900 + 90 + 5 = 995

51

On a math test, you might need the exact answer. But in the real world, it's often okay to estimate, or round, your answer. Find an answer fast by rounding the double or triple digits quickly in your head. Simply round up or down to the nearest whole number.

At the very least, rounding is a good way to check your work because you know the answer should be close to the rounded number.

591 - 123 becomes 600 - 100, which is 500.
So the answer is **"about 500."**

34 + 69 becomes 30 + 70, which is 100.
So the answer is **"about 100."**

Multiply double digits in your head
using the rainbow shortcut.

24 x 31 = ?

24 x 31

2 x 3 = 6

Multiply the first numbers together to get the first digit.

24 x 31

4 x 1 = 4

Multiply the second two numbers to get the last digit.

24 x 31

2 x 1 = 2

24 x 31

4 x 3 = 12

Now multiply the outside numbers together.
Then multiply the inside numbers together.

$$12 + 2 = 14$$

Then add them together to get the middle digit.

If the middle digit is more than 10, carry the 1 to the first column.

$$6[14]4 = 744$$

(carry the 1)

$$24 \times 31 = 744$$

This trick is called the rainbow shortcut because of the rainbow-shaped path you take as you multiply digits.

WAKE UP!

You'll happily hop out of bed once you've tried these tricks.

53

Get moving. When you move your body—even just a little bit—you'll start to feel energized. Walking up and down a set of stairs at a normal pace for 10 minutes can help you feel more awake than caffeine does.

54 **Want to guarantee you'll jump out of bed each morning?** Put your alarm clock on the other side of the room. This way, your feet will have to hit the floor if you want the beeping to stop. Now that you're standing, it's more likely that you'll stay up than hop back into bed!

55

Drink a cold glass of water. Most people wake up dehydrated. When you're dehydrated, you feel fatigued. But a glass of water instantly boosts your energy.

56 **Breathe in. Breathe out.** This fast breathing exercise is energizing instead of calming.

1 Start with your elbows bent and your fists in line with your shoulders.

2 Quickly breathe in and raise your fists straight up into the air.

3 Quickly breathe out and return your fists to the first position.

4 Repeat for 30 seconds.

GET RID OF THAT GUNK

57

Eliminate stickiness by rubbing it with olive oil and a soft cloth. This works for temporary tattoos on skin and for labels on bottles and jars.

HICCUP
CURE

58 **Put a stop to hiccups** by holding your breath for a couple of seconds and swallowing.

A hiccup happens when your diaphragm and the muscles between your ribs contract. Then the space between your vocal cords snaps shut and—*hic!*

Why It Works

Holding your breath increases the level of carbon dioxide in your blood, which may keep your diaphragm from contracting. Swallowing is an attempt to trick your brain into focusing on something else—like, "Hey, look over here instead!"

STILL HAVE HICCUPS?

59

Drink water from the opposite side of a cup.
Stand over a sink. Lean forward, and then tip a full glass of water toward you. Put your mouth on the edge that's farthest away from you and sip.

Why It Works

The tilting of your head makes your abdominal muscles contract in a way that should stop your hiccups. Plus, your brain is focusing on trying to drink—instead of on the hiccups—which can actually help stop them!

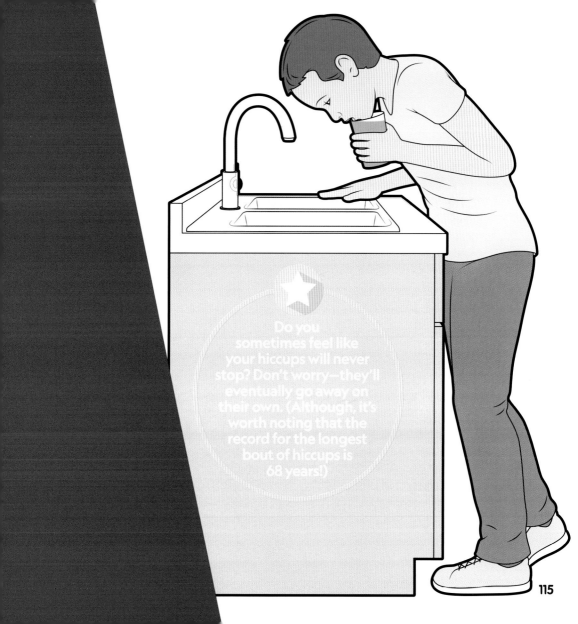

Do you sometimes feel like your hiccups will never stop? Don't worry—they'll eventually go away on their own. (Although, it's worth noting that the record for the longest bout of hiccups is 68 years!)

HACKER HERO

Hacker: Mallory Kievman

Invention: Hiccupops

Mallory Kievman was just 13 years old when she got the worst case of hiccups ever. She was hiccuping for weeks and couldn't get them to stop. She tried every alleged hiccup cure she could find—from drinking pickle juice to eating a spoonful of sugar.

Eventually, Mallory started playing around in her family's kitchen. She took three of her favorite cures—sugar, apple cider vinegar, and lollipops—and created the perfect recipe for stopping the hiccups. And it actually worked!

It took more than 40 attempts to develop a recipe that tastes good, cures the hiccups, and can sit on a store shelf.

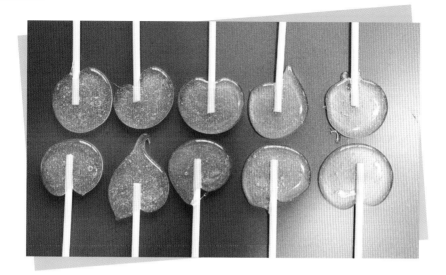

But it was worth all the hard work: Hiccups aren't just annoying. They're also a side effect of a lot of medications for cancer treatments and other serious diseases. That's why Mallory ended up winning an award for her invention. And even better, she gets to help people all over the country!

There is no official cure for the hiccups, and there's no universally agreed-upon way to treat them. That's probably why there are so many remedies out there. Your body might react differently to a "cure" than someone else's will, so it may take some trial and error to find the perfect cure for you.

GET ORGANIZED

Maximize your closet space by repurposing some items you probably already have at home.

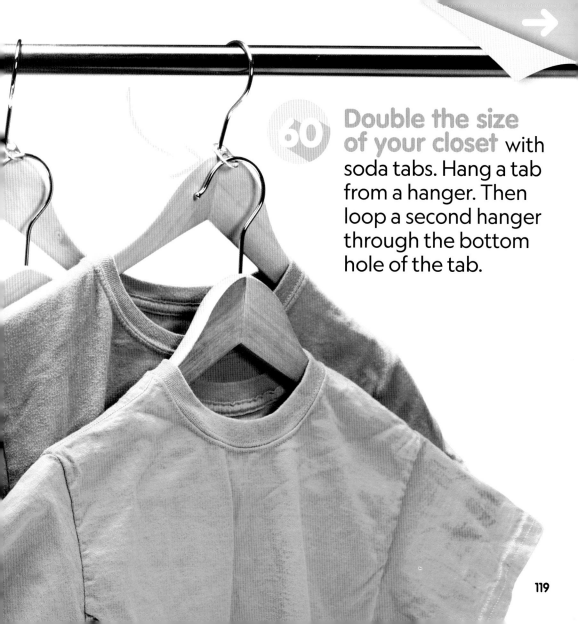

Double the size of your closet with soda tabs. Hang a tab from a hanger. Then loop a second hanger through the bottom hole of the tab.

60

Loop shower hooks
onto the bottom
bar of a hanger.

Now hang hats, belts,
necklaces, tank tops, or
jeans by the belt loops
from the hooks.

NEAT
KNOTS

62

Skip the double-knotted bow! A square knot is one way to tie two ropes of similar thickness together. It's actually a stronger way to tie shoe-laces together, especially if the laces are too short to tie into a bow.

1 Lay the left rope over the right rope in an X position.

2 Wrap the left end over and under the right end, then back up over it.

The square knot is also called the reef knot because it was used to "reef"—or fold in— the sails of boats during strong storms.

3 The left-hand rope is now on the right. Wrap it over, down, and under.

4 Now grab the two pieces on the left side and the two pieces on the right side and pull equally. The knot should tighten in the center.

The square knot is also used in macramé, which is a decorative fabric made by tying ropes into a series of knots.

LOOK, MA!
NO HANDS!

63

No cupholder in the car?
Your shoe might work!

TOOTHBRUSH TRAY

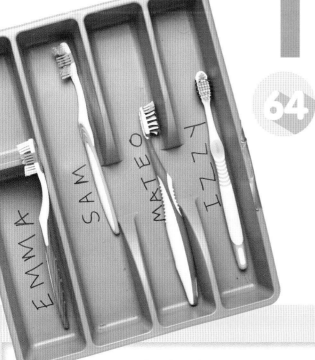

64 **Use a utensil organizer** to tidy toothbrushes and toothpaste in a bathroom drawer. You can even write the name of each family member on the organizer to prevent mix-ups.

kids vs. PLASTIC

This hack upcycles one item and transforms it into another useful item. That means you don't have to buy something new!

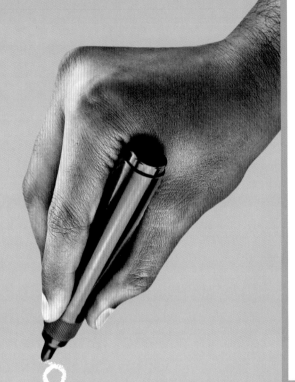

Dry-erase markers work on your mirror! Leave yourself or someone else messages on the bathroom mirror. The markers will wipe off just like on a dry-erase board.

MIRROR MESSAGE

ERASABLE INK

Erase pen ink on paper by dipping a cotton swab into lemon juice. Lightly blot the ink with the juice, but don't use too much or the paper will get soggy.

BYE-BYE, BRAIN FREEZE

67

Don't let a headache ruin your favorite frosty treat. You can vanquish brain freeze by simply pressing your tongue against the roof of your mouth!

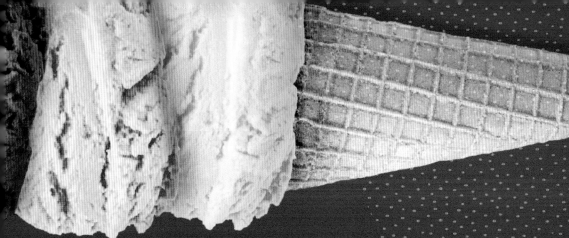

Why It Works

You've probably been there before: One moment, you're carefree, chomping into your favorite flavor of ice cream. And then—zap!—you suddenly have a terrible headache. That's brain freeze, and it happens because of your mouth's sudden change in temperature. So, why the pain? Scientists think the temperature change may cause nearby arteries in the brain to dilate (or expand) and contract (or shrink) very quickly. In turn, your brain responds to those changes by getting a big headache. When you push your tongue against the roof of your mouth, you warm it up and ease the freeze. Now you can get back to enjoying your ice cream. (Just slow down this time!)

CRAFTY CARABINERS

These metal clips are a must-have for true life-hackers!

68

Carry multiple bags with one hand by first looping the bag handles through a carabiner.

Find carabiners online or at sporting goods stores.

Carabiners are used in rock climbing to attach a climber to a rope or a harness. This keeps climbers safe and allows them to clip on and off their ropes quickly and easily.

Keep pairs of shoes together by looping a carabiner through sneaker laces or through the straps of your favorite flip-flops or sandals. Then you can hang the carabiner from the strap of your beach bag or gym bag.

Carabiners are a hacker's dream because they can be used so many ways. How else would you use a carabiner?

70

Keep hair ties organized on a carabiner clip.

FAST FREEZE

71

Get cold water fast! Fill a reusable water bottle a quarter of the way with water and leave it on its side in the freezer. Once it's frozen, fill it with water to take with you while on the go.

REDUCE THE WRAPPING

72

Wrap your sandwich (or a snack) in a bandanna.

It doubles as a napkin while you're eating!

kids VS. PLASTIC

Bandanna sandwich bags are more than just practical—they're good for the planet! Even though plastic sandwich bags can be recycled, they usually need to be brought to a special recycling center, which most people aren't willing to do. That means they end up in the trash. And because they're so lightweight, the wind often blows them out of bins, creating litter that ends up in a landfill—or worse. Overall, it's more difficult to recycle plastics, so it's best to avoid using them in the first place whenever we can.

HACKER HERO

Hacker: Hayat Sindi

Invention: A paper-based tool to diagnose diseases

Many people live in remote places where visiting a doctor or going to a hospital is almost impossible. That means these people can't take tests that could find a disease before it's too late to cure it—or take tests that make sure their body is functioning properly. Scientist Hayat Sindi wanted to change that.

Her invention had to be cheap, lightweight, and easy to use. And it couldn't use electricity. So she created a postage-stamp-size piece of paper that could analyze one drop of bodily fluid like blood, saliva, or urine. Once the fluid touches the paper, chemicals on the paper cause it to change to a certain color. It's easy to read because every color is tied to a different health issue or disease. And each test costs just one penny!

Now people around the world can monitor things like liver function, which helps keep them healthy and safe while they are taking certain medicines. With innovations like Hayat's invention, people around the world can have a chance to be healthy—no matter where they live or how much money they have.

MIRROR,
MIRROR

73

Mirror foggy after a hot shower? Polish it with a small amount of shaving cream and a washcloth. Your mirror will be squeaky-clean for weeks!

This hack also works on eyeglasses or swimming goggles. Clean your lenses with a small amount of shaving cream and a soft washcloth to prevent fog.

Why It Works

It all has to do with condensation—water droplets that collect on a cool surface when humid air comes into contact with it.

When warm moisture from your shower condenses on the cool surface of a bathroom mirror, the mirror gets all foggy. That's because water droplets are curved like fun-house mirrors. They distort your vision.

Lucky for us, shaving cream can change the structure of the water. Thanks to your shaving cream coating, once the water droplets hit the mirror, they'll combine into a single, thin sheet instead of individual droplets. That thin sheet is easier to see through. So you'll spend less time wiping the mirror clean and more time perfecting your hairdo.

PARTY WITH POM-POMS

What you'll need:

8 sheets of tissue paper
(any size or colors will do!)

1 pipe cleaner

Scissors

String

1 Lay your sheets of tissue paper on top of one another.

2 Keeping the stack together, fold the tissue paper into long, 1-inch (2.5-cm) sections, like an accordion. Then hold the paper together, so that it is folded into one long strip.

3 Wrap the pipe cleaner around the middle of the folded tissue paper to hold it in place. Twist it to secure, and trim the pipe cleaner so that it doesn't have a long tail.

4 Cut both ends of your tissue paper stack so that they're rounded.

5

Flip the stack on its side and stretch out its accordion folds, so that it's shaped like a bow tie.

Try stacking different colored tissue paper into one pom-pom stack!

6

Now, spread each tissue layer apart one at a time. Arrange them so that they're shaped like a sphere.

kids
vs. PLASTIC

Balloons are fun at parties, but they're a big problem for the environment. When balloons float off, they have to end up somewhere. Often they wind up in the ocean, where animals can mistake them for food. Paper pom-poms are a fun, festive alternative to single-use balloons—and they're better for the planet!

7

Hang up your pom-pom with string, toss it on the ground, or decorate with it however you choose!

HACK LIKE A PRO:
PUT IT OUT THERE!

Invention competitions are a great way to present your idea to the world and get some feedback.

Don't let that great idea go unnoticed. Why not enter it in a local competition? There are tons of kid inventor competitions across the country. You never know—you could be the next winner! Dreaming up an invention is just the first step. At competitions, inventors have to pitch their idea to judges. This requires some thought and practice! Pitching an idea means giving a short and exciting presentation that shows how the invention works, how it's unique, and why people need it. Inventors have as little as four minutes to say everything they want to say. And an audience is often watching.

You'll also have to share your prototype, or mock-up, of the invention. Then the judges will ask detailed questions. They might be curious about what problem you are solving or why you chose to solve it that way.

In the end, awards are often given for each grade level, as well as in different categories like public safety, home organization, technology, and transportation. There may also be awards for the most patentable invention, the best prototype, or the best pitch.

Competitions are a great way to get feedback on your idea. You'll see your idea in a whole new way. With feedback from experts, you'll be one step closer to turning your invention into a real problem-solving product. How cool is that?!

Winners of local competitions can go on to compete in national competitions like the National Invention Convention and Entrepreneurship Expo.

TERRIFIC T-SHIRT TOTE

75 **Grown out of your favorite T-shirt?**
Give it new life as a one-of-a-kind tote bag! You'll need just a pair of scissors and a few simple steps.

1 Lay your shirt flat on a table.

2 With your scissors, cut the sleeves off of the shirt at the seams.

3 Cut around the collar of the shirt. (Now your tote has straps!)

4 Keeping the front and back of the shirt together, make several 1-inch (2.5-cm) cuts along the bottom seam. This should give your shirt fringe.

5 Tie the pieces of fringe you created into knots, using one piece of fringe from the front of the shirt and one from the back for each knot. Keep tying knots until the bottom of the shirt is completely tied shut.

If you're not a fan of fringe, you can always flip your bag inside out. That way the knots will be hidden on the inside! (If you do this, make sure to start with your shirt inside out on step 1 so your bag is right side out at the end.)

PACK YOUR BAG

Keep your backpack organized so you don't lose important stuff.

76

Repurpose a reusable toothbrush holder to store pencils. Write your name on the outside, so you never lose track of your pencils again.

77 **Color-code the tops of your notebooks using highlighters, crayons, or markers.** Draw a stripe on the top edge of each notebook so you can see which is which from above. Now you won't have to dig through your backpack to find the right one!

Staying organized is important. Clutter can make you feel stressed and make it harder for you to focus. A clean space can make you feel relaxed, and being organized can even make you healthier.

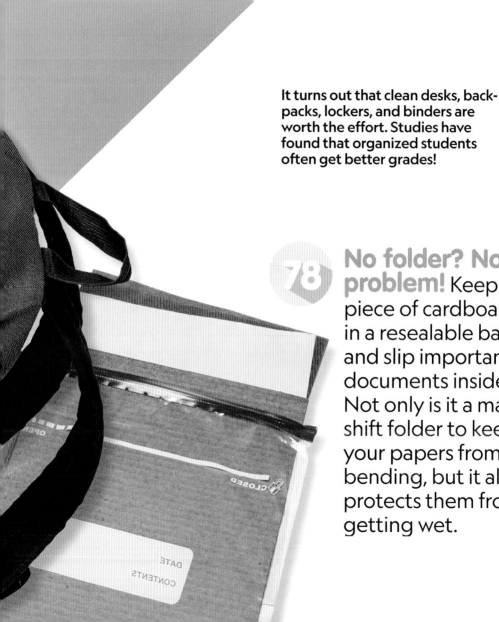

It turns out that clean desks, backpacks, lockers, and binders are worth the effort. Studies have found that organized students often get better grades!

78 **No folder? No problem!** Keep a piece of cardboard in a resealable bag and slip important documents inside. Not only is it a makeshift folder to keep your papers from bending, but it also protects them from getting wet.

BACKYARD, HACK-YARD!

These outdoorsy DIYs will make your backyard blossom.

Birdbaths aren't just for show. According to one study, birds that had recently bathed were better fliers. That means they're harder for predators to catch!

79

Make a bird-bath out of old pots.
This is a simple way to make your yard an avian oasis. If you have large empty pots hanging around, just flip them over and stack them up. Then balance a large plate—the kind you put under a pot to catch water drainage—on top for the bird-bath. Fill it with water, and you're done!

80

Build a compost pile. In the United States, food scraps and waste make up about 30 percent (or more!) of all garbage. But they don't need to go to the landfill—they can be turned into fertilizer that helps plants grow. How? Composting!

Here's what to do:

With an adult, choose somewhere in the yard—like a back corner—for your compost pile. Section it off, and place a bin there. Put your ingredients in the bin. You'll need an equal amount of dry brown stuff (like old pine needles) and fresher green stuff (like grass clippings or veggie scraps). Layer the different items, add some soil or already-made compost to the top, and then sprinkle the pile with water to add moisture.

No backyard? No problem. You can compost food scraps in containers at home. And—get this—a healthy compost pile shouldn't even stink. *Whew!*

What can be composted?

fruits
vegetables
eggshells
coffee grounds
paper
dryer lint
cotton rags
leaves
grass clippings

SHORT
STACK

81 Shuffle your cards like a pro.

1 Stack the cards and then separate them into two piles with the numbers facing down.

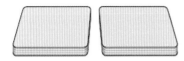

2 Grab each pile. Your thumb should be on one side, your middle and ring finger on the other side, and your pointer finger on top.

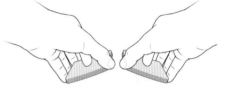

3 Lift the inside corner of each stack using your thumb.

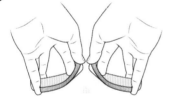

4 Now riffle just the corners of the two decks together by letting the cards fall from your thumb as they intersperse between each other.

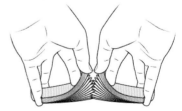

5 Now push the two decks together.

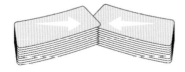

CAMPFIRE CRAVINGS

Making s'mores? Remove a roasted marshmallow from a stick without getting your hands messy. You'll need a friend to help.

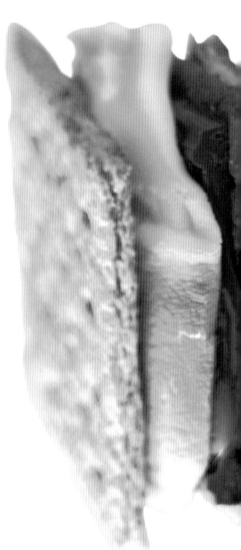

Always grab an adult before making a fire!

Here's what to do:

One person steps away from the fire with the roasted marshmallow still on the end of the stick. The other person holds one half of a graham cracker in each hand (don't forget to put the chocolate piece on one of the halves). That person places a cracker on either side of the marshmallow, squishes the crackers together, and slides the marshmallow off the stick. Now you're ready to snack!

FAKE IT TILL YOU MAKE IT

Hack your mood with body language tricks!

83 Force a smile. Any smile, including a fake one, will actually make you feel happier.

Why It Works

Turning your frown upside down tricks your brain into releasing hormones that help your mood and reduce your stress levels. Even a forced smile will have the same results! Smiling can also boost your immune system.

84

Don't slump! Good posture can help you feel more confident. Keep your back straight, your shoulders pulled back, and your head held high when you're sitting, standing, or walking. You'll look and feel more confident.

Why It Works

Studies have found that our mind affects our body and our body affects our mind. So simply acting like we are more confident can make us feel more confident. Also, we feel taller when we practice good posture, which makes us feel more powerful.

PAPER CLIP
PERFECTION

85

Draw a perfect circle with a simple trick.

What you'll need:

A paper clip

Two pencils

A sheet of paper

1 Unfold the paper clip by pulling the inside loop up and over until it lays flat.

2 Place one pencil in each crook of the paper clip.

3 Hold one pencil in place. Then spin the other pencil in a clockwise direction. *Ta-da!* A perfect circle.

PROTOTYPE (IM)PERFECTION

After you get a great idea, it's time for the next step.

You have an idea for a product. Now what? Build a prototype, of course! A prototype serves as a model for a future product or machine. It's a way for inventors to see their idea come to life. While building a prototype, an inventor might realize that there's a problem with their idea, or they might think of a cool new feature to add to their product.

Prototypes don't have to be perfect, but they're usually built to scale. They could be a miniature version, built in the correct proportions. Or they could be life-size. For example, a prototype of a shoe could actually fit onto your foot, but a prototype of an amusement park ride might be small enough to sit on top of a dining room table.

Sometimes, prototypes work like the product will. Other times, they might just show what something will look like. An inventor might make a prototype of a car that is miniature in size and doesn't actually have an engine or wheels that turn. And that's okay! The important part is that we can imagine what the idea will be like!

AN AIR PROTOTYPE PRESENTED IN 2019

In 2019, a German company presented a prototype for an air taxi—a vehicle that picks you up like a cab, but flies!

WRIGHT BROTHERS' PLANE

Some inventors get inspired by ideas that came before them. The Wright brothers are credited with inventing the first airplane in the early 1900s, but Leonardo da Vinci sketched a flying machine way back in the early 16th century. It had flapping wings like a bird. There was just one issue—it didn't work!

SPLISH-
SPLASH!

86

DIY a backyard sprinkler
with an upcycled soda bottle, a
hose, and some duct tape.

What you'll need:
Two-liter soda bottle
Pushpin
Duct tape
Hose

1 Using the pushpin, poke a bunch of small holes into one side of the bottle. Leave an inch or two (2.5 to 5 cm) between each hole.

2 Insert a hose into the opening of the bottle and secure it with duct tape.

3 Make sure the side of the bottle with the holes is facing up. Turn on the hose and *voilà!*

Why It Works

Water flows from the hose into the soda bottle, but it has no way to escape! The exit has been duct-taped closed—except for the holes you made in the bottle! The water pressure builds and pushes the water up through the holes. Try covering a few of them with your fingers. The water should shoot even higher out of the remaining holes!

BRRR...

Chill out with these freezing hacks.

87 Make your own flexible ice pack by adding one part rubbing alcohol to three parts water in a resealable plastic bag. Place it in your freezer to cool.

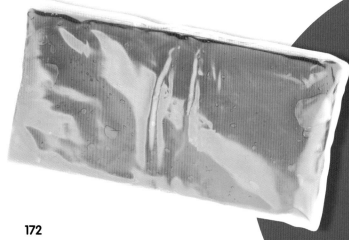

Why It Works
Why doesn't this ice pack freeze completely? It's because rubbing alcohol has a much lower freezing point than water does. Your freezer doesn't get cold enough to turn the rubbing alcohol and water mix into ice.

Make a soda cold fast!

Submerge the can in a bowl of ice, topped off with water and a lot of salt.

Why It Works

If you placed the can in the freezer, it would take about 20 minutes to get cold. But placing the can in ice, water, and salt reduces the chill time drastically. The key to coolness? Salt. It lowers the freezing point of water from 32°F (0°C) to as low as minus 6°F (-21°C). That's why we put salt on roads and sidewalks in the winter. Basically, salt makes water become colder, instead of just letting it turn into ice. The amount of salt you need will depend on how many drinks you want to cool. For one drink in a bowl, start with one big table-spoon of salt.

EAT YOUR VEGGIES ...
AGAIN.

89

Don't throw away your food scraps just yet! Some store-bought veggies will regrow in just a glass of water.

After cutting the tops off, stick the white bottoms and roots of a bundle of green onions into a little glass of water and watch them regrow. Chop the new onions and repeat. You can grow them over and over again!

Try regrowing romaine lettuce the same way, too!

TURN UP THE HEAT!

These cool tips will make you a cold-weather pro.

90 JUMP!

Why It Works

Do about 25 jumping jacks before you go outside. That should be just enough to increase the heart rate and blood flow to your muscles, but not enough to make you break a sweat. Sweat will cool you down and dampen your clothing, which you want to keep dry.

91

SAY "N⌀" TO HOT COCOA.

Why It Works

Though you may be tempted to grab a hot chocolate when you're shivering, drink room temperature water instead. A too-hot drink sends a signal to your body that it's time to cool down—the exact opposite of what you want!

COOL IT!

Feeling the heat? Try these hacks to keep cool.

92 APPLY AN **ICE PACK, DAMP WASHCLOTH,** OR **WET BANDANNA** TO YOUR PULSE POINTS.

Why It Works

The goal is to cool down your blood as fast as you can, and pulse points are areas of your body where blood vessels are closest to your skin. Try inside your wrists, elbows, and knees, as well as the back of your neck and the tops of your bare feet.

93 TAKE A WARM SHOWER.

Why It Works

A cold shower cools down our skin temperature, but sends a signal to our bodies to hang on to the heat inside our core. A warm shower increases blood flow to the skin (and makes our body think we're standing outside on a hot day), which leads to heat loss in our core. That cools our entire body down!

MILK-SHAKE

Got five minutes? You can make
some ice cream! Here's how.

What you'll need:

1 cup (240 mL) half-and-half (or whole milk)

2 tbsp (25 g) sugar

1/2 tsp (2.5 mL) vanilla

Quart-size resealable bag

Gallon-size resealable bag

Ice

1 cup (230 g) kosher salt

1

Add the half-and-half (or milk), sugar, and vanilla to the quart-size bag. Seal tightly.

2

Fill the gallon-size bag three-quarters of the way with ice. Add the salt.

3

Put the smaller bag into the larger bag. Seal it tightly.

4

Shake the bag for five minutes. Ask friends and family to help! (You might want to wear gloves or wrap it in a towel.)

5

Remove the small bag from the salty ice water. Scoop into a bowl and enjoy!

Why It Works

Even though there is no salt in the ice cream itself, salt is an important part of the ice-cream-making process. Just as in the cold-can hack on page 173, salt helps the liquid freeze more quickly. That's how you can get ice cream in just five minutes!

But adding salt isn't just about eating your ice cream ASAP. When the milk, sugar, and vanilla mixture freezes fast (in other words—with salt), the ice cream forms smaller ice crystals instead of larger ones. That makes it soft and creamy.

HACK LIKE A PRO:
JOIN A HACKATHON!

When people say, **"It's not a sprint; it's a marathon,"** it means that a slow and steady approach is better than acting fast and furious. When it comes to solving problems, slow and steady is usually a safe bet. After all, it can take years to come up with the perfect solution. But sometimes a fast and furious approach can be fun. That's where hackathons come in. They're sprint-like events where a problem has to be solved within a set time limit—sometimes 24 hours or less. It can get competitive! The event is usually themed around a specific dilemma. People form small groups and then tackle the issue together. Some hackers brainstorm all night to try to come up with the best idea.

Many hackathons have to do with technology. So you'll see a group of people sitting around a table, each of them with a laptop. They might be developing a new app or website or hardware like a cool drone. Some hackathons aim to tackle a citywide or statewide problem, like reducing traffic, increasing recycling, or improving grades in schools.

Sometimes the problem never gets solved—and that's okay! The goal of the hackathon is to make some progress and get one step closer to a solution.

SUPER STICKY

Duct tape has so many creative uses.
Which one is your favorite?

95

Want your stuff to stand out from the rest? Create duct tape decals! You can decorate your bike, notebooks, water bottles—whatever. Try cutting shapes from duct tape to use as stickers. You can even try glow-in-the-dark duct tape.

Duct tape was originally called duck tape because water slid off it like it slides off a duck's feathers.

96

Slipping and sliding around the house? Stick some duct tape onto the bottom of some slippery socks. The added friction will keep you from sliding. It's like a DIY pair of slippers!

Make a duct tape tag.

It won't rip like paper, and it's waterproof. Use it as a gift tag, a backpack charm, or a luggage tag.

What you'll need:
Card stock or paper
Duct tape
Scissors
Hole punch
Ribbon
Permanent markers

1 Cover the front and back of a piece of card stock or paper with rows of duct tape slightly longer than the paper.

2 Cut out various shapes from the sheet of duct tape paper.

TO:

FROM:

3 Use a hole punch to make a hole at the top of each tag. Then loop a thin ribbon through the hole and tie it in a knot. Decorate the tag with permanent markers.

POP STOP

Straws float in a can of soda because of carbonation—carbon dioxide gas in water. Pressure keeps the gas in the water until you release it (when you pop open the tab). That's why all those little bubbles appear in a freshly opened can of soda.

Those bubbles are the culprits that keep your straw from staying put, since they often stick to the outside and inside of the straw.

98 **Stop your straw from floating upward.** Spin the pull tab 180 degrees, and then slip your paper straw through the hole to keep it from floating up.

kids vs. PLASTIC

Americans use hundreds of millions of plastic straws each day. They get used once and then thrown away, and they often end up in the ocean, where fish and other sea creatures can accidentally eat them. But many people are trying to change this. Restaurants, companies, and even entire cities have banned plastic straws. You can help by choosing not to use a straw or by using a paper straw or reusable silicone straw instead.

TISSUE TWINS

99

This one's a must when you have a cold: Using rubber bands or tape, attach an empty tissue box to a full one. When you're done with a tissue, dispose of it in the empty box. So long, icky tissue trash!

CREATE YOUR OWN HACK!

Put on your inventor's cap: What's a trick or tip that you use to make life easier? Or what's a problem that you hope to solve? Is there a way something you do can be done more easily, more simply, better, or faster? There's a hack for everything—even for how to create a hack! If you're feeling stuck, try one of the following tips to hack your mind and think more creatively.

Think opposite. For example, if you're trying to plan the coolest birthday party ever, first think of what would make the worst party ever. It's all about letting the ideas flow—both good and bad ones! We're often too scared to share our ideas because we're afraid of what others might think of them. You never know which "bad" ideas will turn into great things!

101

Switch it up. Sometimes a change is all we need to spark our creativity. If you've been writing, try talking. If you've been talking, try doodling. If you've been doodling, try writing. If you've been inside, go outside. And if you've been outside, head inside! If you've been brainstorming alone, gather some friends. And if you've already been in a group, go solo.

What Is Brainstorming?

Technically, brainstorming is the process of creating ideas or solving problems through group discussions. (But you can generate ideas alone if you'd like!) Usually there is one topic or problem that the group focuses on. Tons of ideas are written down. There are no bad or wrong contributions!

By the end of the brainstorming session, one or two winning ideas are chosen. Regardless of the outcome, the process of brainstorming can be a lot of fun. It's a great exercise in thinking big and getting creative. There are so many problems out there that need solving, inventions that need to be made, and hacks that are waiting to be discovered. So what are you waiting for? Start imagining!

LEARN MORE

kids vs. PLASTIC

Plastic bags, utensils, straws, containers, and bottles are a part of our everyday life. But single-use plastic—plastic that gets used once and then thrown away—can harm the environment. It often ends up in landfills or, even worse, the ocean. Many life hacks can help repurpose, reuse, or recycle plastic items in your life. But the best way to reduce plastic is to stop using it. Here are a few ways you can help.

1 Say **NO** to straws.

2 Fill up a **reusable water bottle** at a water fountain.

Want to reduce plastic in your life? Go to natgeokids.com/KidsVsPlastic and take the Kids vs. Plastic pledge.

3 **Snack on fruit** (it comes in its own wrapper!) instead of packaged snacks.

5 **Never litter—** and recycle any plastic that you do use. Or better yet, upcycle it!

4 When ordering ice cream, **ask for a cone** instead of a cup.

Hack Roundup

1. Make an ice pop drip tray out of a cupcake liner.
2. Peel a banana from the bottom.
3. Make a cupcake sandwich.
4. Reuse old containers as secret storage.
5. Organize jewelry in plastic eggs.
6. DIY beads out of paper.
7. Hack homework with 25-minute study sessions.
8. Organize your notebook with a table of contents.
9. Read homework out loud.
10. Cut a cake with floss, not a knife.
11. Save water by using a dishwasher.
12. Trick out your toilet with a reused water bottle.
13. Cut water waste with a bucket and sponge.
14. Chill out with a calming breathing technique.
15. Make a magnetic cup to hold your stuff.
16. Never lose your keys with a magnetic key ring.
17. Make a bookmark that never falls out of your book.
18. Turn cake mix into cookies.
19. Keep your shoes clean with a shower cap.
20. DIY your own TV with an upcycled sandwich bag.
21. Pack a suitcase like a pro by rolling clothes.
22. Binder clip your money and keys.
23. Binder clip your toothpaste.
24. And binder clip your headphones.
25. Make a lantern out of a water jug.
26. Keep your bandage from falling off.
27. Make chopsticks easier to use with a rubber band.
28. Start a quick campfire with chips.
29. Master your memory with mnemonics ...
30. ... and a memory palace ...
31. ... and repetition.
32. And don't forget to sing.
33. Use your hand and the sun to estimate time until sunset.
34. Make your own gift bag from wrapping paper.
35. Use a drinking glass as a phone speaker.
36. Take a shower to catch some *z*'s.
37. Or slip on some warm socks.
38. Or grab a good book.
39. Use sunglasses as a screen stand.
40. Upcycle an old sock into a cool cozy.
41. Fold your shirts perfectly.
42. Train your brain by learning music.
43. Or another language.
44. Or exercising.
45. Make a perfect pancake.
46. Check your bad breath.
47. Un-stink your room with vanilla.
48. Un-stink your shoes with dryer sheets.
49. Or conquer bad smells with baking soda.
50. Add big numbers in your head.
51. Use rounding to do mental math quickly.

52. Multiply double digits with the rainbow shortcut.
53. Wake up faster by exercising.
54. Move your alarm clock far from your bed.
55. Drink a cold glass of water in the morning to wake up.
56. Try an energizing breathing technique.
57. Use olive oil to get rid of sticky stuff.
58. Cure hiccups by holding your breath and swallowing.
59. Or by drinking from the opposite side of a cup.
60. Use soda pull tabs to double the size of your closet.
61. Use shower hooks to hang your hats.
62. Tie your shoelaces with a square knot.
63. Use a shoe as a car cupholder.
64. Separate your toothbrushes with an upcycled utensil tray.
65. Leave messages on your mirror with dry-erase markers.
66. Erase ink with lemon juice.
67. Stop a brain freeze with your tongue.
68. Carry a bunch of bags using a carabiner.
69. Carry your shoes with a carabiner.
70. And use one to keep your hair ties organized.
71. Get cold water on-the-go.
72. Use a bandanna to wrap a sandwich.
73. Make your mirror fog-proof with shaving cream.
74. DIY planet-friendly pom-poms.
75. Make a tote bag from an old T-shirt.
76. Use an old toothbrush holder to organize pencils.
77. Color-code your notebooks for easy viewing.
78. DIY your own folder.
79. Make a birdbath out of old pots.
80. Compost.
81. Shuffle cards like a pro.
82. Grab a friend to make less-mess s'mores.
83. Force a smile to give yourself confidence.
84. Or sit up nice and tall.
85. Use a paper clip to draw a perfect circle.
86. DIY a sprinkler out of an upcycled soda bottle.
87. Make your own ice pack.
88. Get a soda can cold fast with salt.
89. Regrow green onions in a glass of water.
90. Warm up with exercise.
91. But not with hot cocoa.
92. Cool down by knowing your pulse points.
93. Or taking a warm shower.
94. Make ice cream in a plastic bag— by shaking it really fast.
95. Personalize your stuff with duct tape.
96. Make your socks nonslip with duct tape.
97. Make duct tape tags.
98. Turn a pull tab to keep your straw still.
99. Reuse an old tissue box as a tissue trash can.
100. Embrace your bad ideas.
101. Spark your creativity with change.

Index

Boldface indicates illustrations. If illustrations are included within a page span, the entire span is **boldface.**

Index

Photo Credits

All photos by Mark Thiessen & Becky Hale/NGP unless otherwise noted below:

Cover, Mark Thiessen & Becky Hale/NGP; 4, Hannamariah/Shutterstock; 4 (doodles), pio3/Shutterstock; 7 (bottles), AlenKadr/Shutterstock; 7 (bin), Mike Flippo/Shutterstock; 7 (paper), Roman Samokhin/Shutterstock; 7 (tubes), Guztsudio/Shutterstock; 10, bergamont/Shutterstock; 18, Sora Devore/National Geographic Image Collection; 18-19, Andriy Lipkan/Shutterstock; 19, Rainforest Connection; 21, koosen/Shutterstock; 22 (notepad), sittipong/Shutterstock; 22 (doodles), pio3/Shutterstock; 22 (numbers), chneeEule/Shutterstock; 23, Padma Sanjaya/Shutterstock; 27, Adobe Stock; 29, LedyX/Shutterstock; 30, Andrey Popov/Shutterstock; 31, keerati/Shutterstock; 32 (bubbles), Nataliya Turpitko/Shutterstock; 32 (bucket), Veniamin Kraskov/Shutterstock; 33, Chris Philpot; 34, Amanda Edwards/WireImage/Getty Images; 34 (boxes), New Africa/Shutterstock; 34-35 (basketball, star, music notes, magnifying glass), campincool/Shutterstock; 35 (palm tree, ship wheel), derter/Shutterstock; 35 (music notes), campincool/Shutterstock; 35 (volcano), derGriza/Shutterstock; 39, Lori Epstein/NGP; 42, Shane Trotter/Shutterstock; 44 (eggs), Nattika/Shutterstock; 44 (butter), Robyn Mackenzie/Shutterstock; 44 (baking soda), Gts/Shutterstock; 45 (cookie), CnOPhoto/Shutterstock; 45 (flour), Sarah Marchant/Shutterstock; 45 (sugar), Dynamicfoto/Shutterstock; 49, Callie Broaddus/NGP; 53 (binder clip), vamdesigner/Shutterstock; 56 (Band-Aid), Kitch Bain/Shutterstock; 56 (scissors), Yganko/Shutterstock; 58, Moonnoon/Shutterstock; 58-59 (graph paper), Stephen Marques/Shutterstock; 59, Unlim3d/Dreamstime; 60, Nipaporn Panyacharoe/Shutterstock; 62, vipman/Shutterstock; 65, Irina Mir/Shutterstock; 66, MrIncredible/Shutterstock; 66 (Uranus), David Aguilar; 68 (pencil), photastic/Shutterstock; 68 (circles), Ron Dale/Shutterstock; 68 (yellow lined paper), filo/iStockphoto; 69, Rashad Ashur/Shutterstock; 70 (hand), Prostock-studio/Shutterstock; 70 (grass), Yellowj/Shutterstock; 77, Karen DeMatteo/National Geographic Image Collection; 82, Vitalina Popova/Alamy Stock Photo; 83, Billion Photos/Shutterstock; 89, MSSA/Shutterstock; 92, Chris Tzou/Bloomberg via Getty Images; 92-93 (background), Shuttersv/Shutterstock; 93 (building), Chris Tzou/Bloomberg via Getty Images; 93, Theodore Kaye; 99, FGorgun/iStockphoto/Getty Images; 100 (fabric softener), studiomode/Alamy Stock Photo; 100 (smell), peace_art/Shutterstock; 101, joey333/iStockphoto/Getty Images; 103, Ljupco Smokovski/Shutterstock; 105, Elizabett/Shutterstock; 109, MemoryMan/Shutterstock; 110 (water), Dmitry Naumov/Shutterstock; 110 (clock),

Astarina/Shutterstock; 111, Chris Philpot; 112, ranplett/iStockphoto/Getty Images; 115, Chris Philpot; 116 (LE), Andrew Sullivan/The New York Times/Redux Pictures; 117 (RT), Andrew Sullivan/The New York Times/Redux Pictures; 122, Kristo Robert/Shutterstock; 124, Chris Philpot; 128, cunaplus/AdobeStock; 129, New Africa/Shutterstock; 129, Roman Samokhin/Shutterstock; 130-131, M. Unal Ozmen/Shutterstock; 133, matkub2499/Shutterstock; 137, Lori Epstein/NGP; 140, Rebecca Hale/National Geographic Image Collection; 141, Hayat Sindi/National Geographic Image Collection; 142 (towel), Byjeng/Shutterstock; 142 (foam), Dmitrij Skorobogato/Shutterstock; 143, Dx09/Shutterstock; 149 (LE), Pluto/Alamy Stock Photo; 149 (RT), Xinhua/Alamy Stock Photo; 157, Lori Epstein/NGP; 158, Evan Lorne/Shutterstock; 159 (potatoes), Edward Westmacott/Shutterstock; 159 (pear), bergamont/Shutterstock; 159 (peaches), Tim UR/Shutterstock; 159 (egg shells), amenic181/Shutterstock; 159 (herbs), matkub2499/Shutterstock; 159 (apple), Roman Samokhin/Shutterstock; 159 (leaves), Julia Filipenko/Shutterstock; 159 (onions) Bozena Fulawka/Shutterstock; 159 (wad of paper), Photodisc; 159 (banana), bergamont/Shutterstock; 160, AR Images/Shutterstock; 161, Chris Philpot; 162, Acme Food Arts/Photolibrary RM/Getty Images; 164, Jose Luis Pelaez Inc/Digital Vision/Getty Images; 165, Maria Averburg/Shutterstock; 166 (pencil), Cphoto/Dreamstime; 166 (paper), Garsya/Shutterstock; 166 (paper clip), Jakub Krechowic/Shutterstock; 169 (UP), Armin Weigel/picture alliance via Getty Images; 169 (LO), Apic/Getty Images; 170 (bottle), gvictoria/Shutterstock; 170 (tape), Bjoern Wylezich/Shutterstock; 170 (hose), Photo Melon/Shutterstock; 171, Callie Broaddus/NGP; 172, Niteen Kasle/Alamy Stock Photo; 173, krungchingpixs/Shutterstock; 176, Chistoprudnaya/Shutterstock; 177, Dawn Balaban/Shutterstock; 178, Valentyn Volkov/Shutterstock; 181 (salt), Chones/Shutterstock; 181 (bags), a_v_d/Shutterstock; 181 (ice), Valentyn Volkov/Shutterstock; 181 (milk), Kenishirotie/Shutterstock; 181 (sugar), Anton Starikov/Shutterstock; 181 (vanilla), Noel V. Baebler/Shutterstock; 184, chekart/Shutterstock; 185 (UP), Xavier Galiana/AFP via Getty Images; 185 (LO), Luke MacGregor/Bloomberg via/Getty Images; 195, photastic/Shutterstock; 196-197, pio3/Shutterstock; 199 (ice cream), Kelpfish/Dreamstime; 199 (bottle), Kidsada/Shutterstock; 199 (banana), bergamont/Shutterstock

Published by National Geographic Partners, LLC. All rights reserved. Reproduction of the whole or any part of the contents without written permission from the publisher is prohibited.

Since 1888, the National Geographic Society has funded more than 12,000 research, exploration, and preservation projects around the world. The Society receives funds from National Geographic Partners, LLC, funded in part by your purchase. A portion of the proceeds from this book supports this vital work. To learn more, visit natgeo.com/info.

NATIONAL GEOGRAPHIC and Yellow Border Design are trademarks of the National Geographic Society, used under license.

For more information, visit nationalgeographic.com, call 1-877-873-6846, or write to the following address:

National Geographic Partners
1145 17th Street N.W.
Washington, D.C. 20036-4688 U.S.A.

Visit us online at nationalgeographic.com/books

For librarians and teachers: nationalgeographic.com/books/librarians-and-educators/

More for kids from National Geographic: natgeokids.com

National Geographic Kids magazine inspires children to explore their world with fun yet educational articles on animals, science, nature, and more. Using fresh storytelling and amazing photography, *Nat Geo Kids* shows kids ages 6 to 14 the fascinating truth about the world—and why they should care.

kids.nationalgeographic.com/subscribe

For rights or permissions inquiries, please contact National Geographic Books Subsidiary Rights: bookrights@natgeo.com

Designed by Kathryn Robbins

The publisher would like to thank everyone who made this book possible: Kathryn Williams, Shannon Pallatta, Lori Epstein, Mark Thiessen, Becky Hale, Molly Reid, Anne LeongSon, Gus Tello, and Michelle Harris. And to Michelle Tyler, for her life-hacking talents.

Trade paperback ISBN: 978-1-4263-3908-0
Reinforced library binding ISBN: 978-1-4263-3909-7

Printed in Hong Kong
20/PPHK/1